National Trust

Lytes Cary Manor

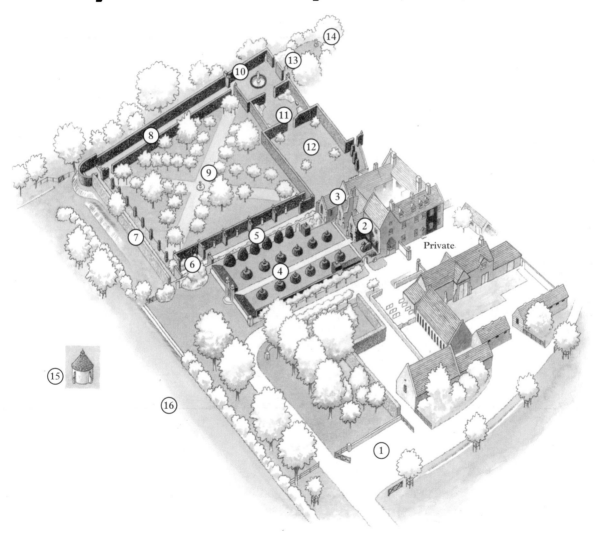

'A place to be remembered'

Philemon Holland on Lytes Cary, 1610

The entrance front in 1835; sepia drawing by J.C. Buckler

One of the blue-and-white Delftware tulip vases in the Great Hall

(*Right*) Tulips illustrated in Henry Lyte's herbal of 1578

(*Opposite*) The Main Border, with the enclosed White Garden beyond

To the outside world, Lytes Cary presents a comfortable jumble of gables, made from the mellow local limestone. They reflect the way the house has grown quietly and gradually over more than 600 years. It is an informal and welcoming place.

From the 14th to the 18th centuries, this was the home of the Lyte family, who gave the place their name and cherished it. The Elizabethan Lytes were botanists and historians, who were fascinated by the story of their own family. They put up coats of arms in the Great Hall and Chapel to record their family connections and to ensure that they were remembered before God. The family's fortunes declined in the 18th century, and in the 1750s they were forced to leave. The house was neglected during the Victorian era, but this meant that it avoided the brutal 'restoration' inflicted on some ancient buildings in the 19th century.

So when Sir Walter Jenner and his wife Flora bought the house in 1907, they acquired a dilapidated, but intact, piece of history. The Jenners belonged to a generation who had been influenced by the Arts and Crafts movement to look at Britain's ancient manor houses with new respect. They lovingly restored the old fabric and added a new family wing, filling both with appropriate furniture and china. Sir Walter bequeathed Lytes Cary to the National Trust in 1949 so that their work would be remembered, and enjoyed by everyone. The National Trust shows the main rooms as they were in the Jenners' time, but has welcomed change in the garden, which the Trust's tenants, Jeremy and Biddy Chittenden, have transformed over 45 years. Lytes Cary is as memorable today as it has ever been.

Key Dates

1255	First mention of William le Lyt
1348	Chantry chapel completed
1460s	Great Hall built by Thomas Lyte
*c.*1500	South wing built
1530s	Great Chamber and Great Parlour created
1578	Henry Lyte publishes his *Niewe Herbal*
1631	Thomas Lyte restores Chapel
1755	Lytes give up estate
1907	Jenners buy and restore house and garden
1949	Sir Walter Jenner gives Lytes Cary to the National Trust
1964	Garden revived by the Chittendens

The Lytes of Lytes Cary

Thomas Lyte in 1611, proudly wearing the Lyte Jewel

James I gave Thomas Lyte this miniature portrait of himself set in an exquisite jewelled locket

The house takes its name from the little river Cary and from the family who lived here for over four centuries. The founder of that family was William le Lyte, who was a feudal tenant of the estate as early as 1286. A tablet in the Chapel shows him and his second wife Agnes on their knees praying to the Virgin Mary. About 1343 their grandson Peter probably built the Chapel, and over the next six generations the Lytes gradually expanded the house around it to match their status as landowning gentry.

Lytes Cary was more or less complete by the early 16th century, when John Lyte created comfortable new family rooms in the south range, and 'new built the Hall oriall [the Oriel Room], the 2 great portches, the closetts, the kitchen, and divers other places yet extant, with the dayrie house and the chamber over'. In 1558 John made over the house to his eldest son, Henry, bequeathing him 'his best coate of black velvet, … six spoons of silver, an ale cupp and a wynne cup of silver.' He had obviously lived well.

Henry Lyte (c. 1529–1607) was described as 'a most excellent scholar in several sorts of learning'. Perhaps to escape the continual arguments with his step-mother, he retreated to his study, where he devoted himself to botany and genealogy. In 1578 he published the *Niewe Herbal*, his English translation of a famous Flemish herbal written by Rembert Dodoens and illustrated with 870 beautiful woodcuts of the plants described in it. Lyte's own copy of the original still survives, filled with marginal comments that show his deep knowledge of the local Somerset flora. He dedicated the book to Queen Elizabeth

'from my poore house at Lytescarie' and addressed it to 'the friendly and indifferent reader'. One of these readers was almost certainly the young William Shakespeare, whose plays are full of plant lore. In *The Light of Britayne* (1588) Henry suggested that the British were descended from the ancient Trojans of Homer's epic by comparing similar-sounding place names in Britain and Asia Minor. The title was probably a pun on Lyte's name, and the book was meant more as a literary conceit than as serious history. He presented a copy to the Queen on the day she went to St Paul's to give thanks for the country's deliverance from the Spanish Armada.

Henry's son Thomas (1568?–1638), who succeeded to the estate in 1607, shared his father's fascination with genealogy. So when he repaired the Chapel in 1631, he added the frieze of family coats of arms. He also compiled two very elaborate family trees of the Lytes and another tracing James I's descent from Brutus, the traditional founder of the Roman Republic. The King was so pleased with Thomas's efforts that he presented him with a miniature of himself set in a locket of gold and diamonds. Thomas had himself painted wearing this masterpiece of Jacobean jewellery, which still survives in the British Museum.

The Lytes looked forward as well as back. Thomas's younger step-brother, Henry, was a pioneering advocate of the decimal system, publishing a book on the subject in 1619. Descendants included Col. William Light (1784–1839), founder of the city of Adelaide, and the Rev. Henry F. Lyte (1793–1847), author of the hymn 'Abide with Me!'.

The Lyte family continued to live quietly at Lytes Cary for the next hundred years, but by the mid-18th century they were in serious financial difficulties. Thomas Lyte was in such debt that he had no choice but to put the estate in the hands of trustees, and then to mortgage it. Finally, on 25 March 1755 he and his son John surrendered all their rights to their ancestral home. Tenants moved into the house, which gradually fell into decay. In 1810 a neighbour reported that the north range had 'lately been destroyed and a farm house built on the site'. By the time John Buckler came to draw the house in 1835, the west range had also disappeared, and the future for the rest of Lytes Cary looked grim.

Carnations from Henry Lyte's *Niewe Herbal*

(*Above left*) The botanist Henry Lyte holding a copy of his *Niewe Herbal* (1578), which is on display in the Great Hall

(*Left*) The garden front in 1835; sepia drawing by J.C. Buckler

The Jenners

Sir Walter Jenner and his wife Flora bought what was left of Lytes Cary in 1907. His father, Sir William Jenner, had been Queen Victoria's doctor, and though an expert on typhoid, had been unable to save Prince Albert when he caught the disease in 1861. His uncle Charles had founded the famous Edinburgh department store that bears their name. Like most of his brothers, Sir Walter had an army career, serving in the 9th Lancers throughout the First World War, when he was mentioned in dispatches three times and awarded the DSO.

In 1907, when he was 47, Sir Walter was looking for somewhere to settle in the West Country. His brother Leopold had just bought Avebury Manor, a very similar house in the next county (now also in the care of the National Trust). William Morris and the Arts and Crafts movement had opened the Jenners' eyes to the charms of mellow Tudor manor houses like Lytes Cary and Avebury. When Sir Walter arrived at Lytes Cary, he found the Great Hall being used as a cider store, and the Great Parlour was full of farm equipment. But he could see its possibilities.

An earlier generation would probably have cut out all the crumbling stonework and refaced the entire building in a single style. But Sir Walter appreciated the patina of the ancient Blue Lias stone and the building's gradual evolution. So he asked his architect C.E. Ponting to rebuild the north and west ranges in an unassuming William and Mary style, as later generations of the Lytes might have done, if they had had the money. The most substantial new rooms were the library and the dining room, which was designed to show full-length late 17th-century portraits. He left the historic core of the house more or less untouched. Indeed, he tried to return it to its original form by inserting a traditional Gothic screen in the Great Hall. Unpainted, unpolished woodwork and faded tapestries provided a suitable setting for the old oak and walnut furniture they acquired from dealers like Angel of Bath. The aim was not to create historically precise 'period rooms', but to evoke – in a much more subtle way – an atmosphere of

The ivy-clad Lytes Cary in the early 20th century, before it had been restored by the Jenners

Sir Walter Jenner, who, with his wife Flora, rescued Lytes Cary from Victorian dereliction and gave it to the National Trust

The Little Chamber, which Sir Walter used as his bedroom

age and gradual accumulation, which had disappeared when the Lytes left. A key element were the new seat covers and other embroideries sewn by Sir Walter's sister-in-law in a vaguely 17th-century style.

Patricia Spear, who worked for Sir Walter in the 1940s, remembered him as 'always spick and span.... He used to wear a monocle and when he came close to one he would put his monocle in his eye and give one a very direct look'. His brown boots were always kept shone to a fine army polish. But he was also a considerate employer, whose main recreations were music, the garden and the family's many pets. The Jenners led a quiet existence, visiting friends, playing tennis in the summer, and hunting in the winter.

The Jenners' life at Lytes Cary was overshadowed by a double tragedy. Their first child, Kentish, had died in 1900 when only a month old. Their second, Esmé, was a keen huntswoman, who was Master of the Sparkford Vale Harriers from 1931 to 1932, when she died of pneumonia after a day out hunting, at the age of only 37. Her memorial in the church is inscribed simply, 'My little world'.

It was probably the lack of an heir that decided Sir Walter to pass the house to the National Trust on his death in 1948.

The National Trust

Sir Walter bequeathed Lytes Cary to the Trust in order 'to commemorate the restoration of Lytes Cary after years of neglect so as once again to render the same fit for habitation and also to perpetuate the memory of my wife, my daughter and myself, all of whom devoted such care and energy to that end'. The National Trust therefore shows the main rooms in the old part of the house as the Jenners restored and furnished them, but lets out the rest so that Lytes Cary can remain a family home. From 1955 until his death in 1997 the tenant was Jeremy Chittenden, who, with his wife Biddy, devoted half a lifetime to transforming the garden (p.14). That it is today in such good heart is a testament to all their imagination and hard work.

The Jenners' daughter Esmé, who was a keen huntswoman

Flora, Lady Jenner

7

Tour of the House

A pair of unusual leather figures flanks the fireplace in the Great Hall

The 18th-century birdcage in the Oriel Room

(*Opposite*) The Great Hall

The Screens Passage

You enter the house via the screens passage, which in medieval times divided the Great Hall on the left from the Kitchen and servants' quarters on the right. But all is not quite as it seems: Sir Walter inserted the wooden screen and gallery only in 1907, basing the decoration of the panelling on that in the arch of the Oriel Room.

The Great Hall

This was the main communal space in the medieval house, where the whole household would have eaten on feast days, with the Lytes and favoured guests seated on the dais at the far end. When Sir Walter arrived, he found the room occupied by a cider press and racks of apples. The great glory of the room is the mid-15th-century open roof. The three tiers of curved wind-braces are a typical West Country feature, and are both decorative and practical, relieving the diagonal stresses on the roof caused by Somerset gales.

At the base of each main rafter, an angel supports a shield decorated with the Lyte arms, which also appear in the early 16th-century stained glass in the windows below. In the early 20th century the family historian Sir Henry Maxwell-Lyte returned this heraldic glass, which at some point had been removed from the Great Parlour and Chapel Room.

Furnishings

Sir Walter Jenner collected the mostly 17th-century oak furniture, which reflects changes in eating habits. The long refectory table on the dais was a type developed in the 15th century for communal dining in Great Halls like this one. However, such tables are too heavy to move easily, and so were gradually replaced by more portable, folding tables, like the gateleg, circular one in the middle of the room, which was used for the more intimate meals that became fashionable in the late 17th century. In the cabinet on this table is displayed a copy of Henry Lyte's famous *Herbal* (1578), which catalogued and illustrated the plants of his era (see p.4).

The blue-and-white Delftware pyramid vases on the far table were made in the late 17th century for displaying tulips and other flowers In the 1630s the 'tulipomania' craze had sparked off a speculative frenzy among Dutch bulb collectors.

The two leather figures flanking the fireplace are wearing 17th-century costume, but were probably made in the 18th century and may have belonged to the Lytes. They are somewhat similar to the flat wooden 'dummy-boards' found in some country houses, which may have been used to exaggerate the size of a room or even to discourage burglars. But their exact purpose remains a puzzle.

At the far end of the room on the left is the Oriel Room.

The Oriel Room

This was added to the Great Hall in the early 16th century to provide a more intimate room where the family could eat in private away from their servants. It would originally have been separated from the Great Hall by a wooden screen that slotted into the arch; the grooves for it can still be seen in the stone.

The portrait, dated 1590, over the fireplace depicts Lady Catherine Neville and is attributed to Robert Peake. The birdcage in the form of a house is probably 18th-century.

The embroidered mirror frame in the Great Parlour includes a view of Lytes Cary at the top left

(*Above*) This small window, or squint, allows one to look from the Chapel Room into the Chapel

(*Right*) The Great Parlour

(*Opposite*) The niche in the Little Parlour is filled with 18th- and 19th-century engraved glass

The Chapel Room

The small window (or squint) on the left looks into the Chapel: hence the name of the room. In pre-Reformation times, the family would have observed the celebration of the Mass from here.

The early 17th-century walnut plaque depicts *St Michael vanquishing the Devil*. According to the Book of Revelation, 'Then war broke out in heaven. Michael and his angels waged war upon the dragon [symbolising the devil].... So the great dragon was thrown down, that serpent of old'. There is also a 19th-century view of Greenwich, showing the Royal Naval Hospital designed by Sir Christopher Wren in 1694.

The Great Parlour

In the early 16th century the Lytes added this sunny room overlooking the garden, which was the main family sitting room on the ground floor. In the early 17th century Thomas Lyte put up the panelling, which kept out the draughts and brought a touch of classical dignity to the room.

Sir Walter found the room being used as a store for farm implements. He stripped later layers of paint off the panelling to reveal the original wood. The little internal porch was another draught-excluding device found at Montacute and many other Elizabethan houses.

Furnishings
The mirror by the door has a frame with original 17th-century stumpwork, and panels in the same style embroidered by Sir Walter's sister-in-law, who incorporated views of Lytes Cary and her own house at Avebury Manor. The walnut chairs, which were probably made in Italy around 1700, are also covered with Mrs Jenner's needlework. The other furniture is mainly early 18th-century.

Go through the porch door and turn left down the corridor and left again into the Little Parlour.

The Little Parlour

Henry and Thomas Lyte may have used this little room as a study in which to pursue their historical researches.

The pictures include portraits of Sir Walter in 1940 and of his only child, Esmé, who is shown out hunting. The latter portrait was painted posthumously, in 1932. The horseshoe-shaped table of about 1810 was designed for convivial drinking by the fireside. The curtain on a brass rail screened off the worst of the heat, while keeping the bottles of wine at the right temperature.

Return along the corridor and climb the spiral staircase to the Great Chamber.

Nathan rebukes David for stealing another man's wife by telling the parable of the poor man's ewe lamb, which was stolen by the rich man; detail from the 17th-century Flemish tapestry in the Great Chamber

The Chapel

(*Opposite*) The Great Chamber

The Great Chamber

John Lyte created this impressive room in the 1530s, when he represented Henry VIII's government in Somerset. He showed his loyalty to the King by prominently displaying the royal coat of arms and Tudor roses in the plasterwork on the end wall. His own arms, which feature swans, appear, with those of his wife, Edith Horsey, on the ceiling and on the outside of the bay window.

John Lyte went to such trouble over the decoration, because he reserved the room for his most honoured guests, but the four-poster bed, panelling and tapestries, which emphasise its important status, date from a later, 17th-century era. The Flemish tapestry on the fireplace wall depicts *Nathan reproving David with the story of the poor man and his ewe lamb*. The miniature 18th-century Dutch display cabinet on the left contains a collection of appropriately small Regency porcelain – probably a travelling salesman's samples.

Pass through the ante-room at the far end to the little bedroom.

The Bedroom next to the Great Chamber

This was probably intended as a dressing room rather than a separate bedroom, as the only access is through the Great Chamber. The unusual early 19th-century collapsible bed was designed for soldiers to take on campaign. It recalls Sir Walter's own army days.

Return to the Great Chamber and walk along the first-floor corridor.

The Little Chamber

Sir Walter used this as his bedroom. Patricia Spear remembers having to bring him a breakfast tray every morning at 6. When James Lees-Milne came to discuss the transfer of Lytes Cary to the National Trust, he found Sir Walter in bed and still in his night cap.

The bed came from Burton Pynsent in Somerset. The hangings are modern damask, but the structure is original, of about 1750–75, and may have been slept in by William Pitt the Elder, who was given the house in 1765 by an admirer of his achievements as prime minister.

The portrait of Flora, Lady Jenner was painted in 1893, the year she married Sir Walter.

Leave the house by the front door and turn right to reach the Chapel.

The Chapel

Unlike most country-house chapels, there is no direct link with the house, which it predates. The Chapel was completed in 1348, and was thoroughly renovated in 1631 by Thomas Lyte, who installed the present roof and the frieze painted with the arms of the Lytes and their relations. It was designed as a chantry chapel, where masses could be said for the souls of the family, living and dead.

In 1912 Sir Walter added the stained glass, including medieval glass said to have come from Charlton Mackrell church, which William Le Lyte had commissioned before his death in 1316. William is also commemorated by the tablet to the right of the altar.

The Garden

Not surprisingly, Henry Lyte the herbalist 'had a pretty good collection of plants for that age', according to the 17th-century antiquary John Aubrey, but all trace of his garden has long since disappeared. His son Thomas kept a very well stocked orchard, which in 1618 included 'Apples, 3 skore severall sorts. Pears and Wardens [a type of pear], 44 sorts. Plummes, 15 divers kynds. Grapes, 3 severall sortes. Cherries, 1. Walnuts, 3. Peaches, 1.' The garden probably remained more practical than ornamental during the 17th and 18th centuries, and ran to seed as the house declined in the Victorian period.

The Jenners had to start from scratch. In 1907 they laid out the bones of the present garden to the east and south of the house. They created a grid of more or less rectangular 'garden rooms' and straight walks, each different in size and mood, and divided by high yew hedges and stone walls to create shelter and intrigue. The Lytes Cary garden was much indebted to the Arts and Crafts style popularised by Thomas Mawson and in particular to the garden that Leopold Jenner was creating at Avebury. The Jenners had a garden staff of four.

Graham Stuart Thomas, the National Trust's first Gardens Adviser, designed the Main Border in 1965, after the Chittendens had suggested opening the garden to visitors. In 1996 Biddy Chittenden completely rethought and replanted this border, using a mixture of new and existing plants, but always strictly following Stuart Thomas's original colour scheme. In 1999 she also replanted the White Garden, again blending original shrubs with new ideas.

(*Above*) Roses in the White Garden

(*Right*) The Main Border

Tour of the Garden

The Apostle Garden

Aligned on the front door and the water tower (built in imitation of the Avebury Manor dovecote), this formal approach takes its name from the twelve yew bushes planted by the Jenners that flank the agreeably undulating stone path. The planting against the house is deliberately low-key and simple so as not to distract from the beauty of the building.

Pass through the door in the wall to the left of the Chapel to reach the Main Border.

The Main Border

This is the floral highlight of the garden. The 35-metre-long mixed border moves from blues and yellows, through creams and apricots, to pinks and mauves, reaching a rousing climax of bright pinks and reds. It comprises roses, shrubs and perennials against a backdrop of climbing roses and clematis on a beautiful south-facing wall. The separate White Garden beyond makes a restful contrast.

The Raised Walk

The raised walk offers views down over the orchard – an idea copied from Avebury. A golden thread of *Hypericum calicymum* runs between the tall columns of Irish yew.

The Long Walk

A plain green corridor of grass and yew forms the third side of the Orchard. It is reminiscent, on a smaller scale, of the famous Long Walk at Hidcote in Gloucestershire.

Biddy and Jeremy Chittenden, who transformed the garden over 40 years

The Apostle Garden takes its name from the twelve yew bushes that line the front path. The vista is aligned on the water-tank, which the Jenners modelled on a traditional circular dovecote

The Orchard

Four 'houses' of Weeping Ash were planted at the corners of the Orchard in 1973 to replace Weeping Elms which had succumbed to disease. Quinces, medlars, crab apples and other fruit trees are underplanted with fritillaries and narcissus, which provide a carpet of colour in spring. In the Jenners' day, the servants were strictly forbidden from picking the fruit.

The Pond Garden, Seat Garden and Croquet Lawn

Gaps in the hedges between these three linked gardens were made in the late 1960s, creating a vista to the bay window of the south front. The four arbutuses were always intended to be the focal point of corner beds in the Seat Garden, but this was achieved only in 2001, when box hedges were planted round the new borders.

The Hornbeam Arch and Vase Garden

A tunnel of hornbeam links the Pond Garden to the intimate and peaceful Vase Garden, which contains variegated weigela, underplanted with euphorbia and vinca – another inspired creation of Graham Stuart Thomas.

The Park

You approach the house along a drive, lined with young lime trees, which replace the ancient elms that dominated the park until the 1970s. The gentle parkland setting and the sheep that crop the grass immediately set the tone of informality, which is such a feature of Lytes Cary. Humps and bumps hint at the park's archaeological importance: the remains of a Roman villa and the Roman Fosseway have been discovered here.

The Pond Garden